八卦掌戰勁

The Baguazhang Jin of War

by
Peter Hainzl

Chapter Zero:

Not all things to do with martial arts can be easily understood. It takes a few goes around the mulberry bush for things to start making sense. And that is only if they are meant to make sense. While this is the nature of baguazhang, sometimes it easier to just say, "Fuck it." And treat it all like one big adventure story with you, the protagonist, being the only one who doesn't know what's going on.

And while this is true up to a point, behind the scenes a baguazhang practitioner will be slowly sliding from not knowing what is going on to being in more like a state of pretending to not know what is going on. Even if the idea of pretending does not sit well with a person's psyche, at some point along that same journey (as implied above) the baguazhang practitioner-cum-master will have a tendency to become a hidden dragon.

And that is where the baguazhang journey for most practitioners ends. Unless, of course, one's journey leads them back to true China. Not the theme park version that is in place now that seeks to turn the country into some vanilla version of itself, but the one that is the multilayered culturally diverse China that is a multiverse in itself.

The 'China' of the martial artist is aware that references to turtles are usually implied as insults, while at the same time there is nothing wrong with having stone statues of turtles adorning one's abode because they symbolise the Chinese god of martial arts: The Xuanwu Shangdi.

For those of you not comfortable with the idea of him being a god, think of him as the patron saint or archangel representing Kung Fu.

And so, just for fun, I call upon this mighty warrior as we embark on this quest through uncharted territories in search of this elusive power known as jingong.

Chapter One:

玄

Once upon a time, in a land far far away, there lived a man who wanted to become a martial arts master. And so, when he finally got his act together in his early thirties after years of bullshitting himself like most young men, he embarked on his martial arts journey through the internal Chinese martial art of Baguazhang.

At some point along the journey while doing Baguazhang, he realised that he was also doing qigong. And so he delved deeper into the mysteries of Baguazhang qigong until there was no way to hide it, and he became what he was: The master of it.

And so, along with some Taoist truths and a bit of other crazy shit thrown in, which you can read about in my other books like **The Baguazhang Art of War** and **The Baguazhang Tao of War**, the journey around Baguazhang is meant to end there.

Except... (And this is a big exception)...

Except, and let's just say it on a spiritual level, he eventually finds himself in a situation where despite all of his wanderings, it all comes to naught because he doesn't know about Jingong. Fuck!

Jingong. Yup. That old chestnut. A mysterious power that few have heard of, and yet we all seem to know about it. A secret that is only taught to a select few by masters in the know. But who are apparently unable to clearly express or define it, when pressed for details.

But then I came along. And homie don't play that game. I love mysteries. And if there is a back door to a back room, I will find it and penetrate its darkness. I detest invisible barriers put up to keep people like me out. It's like having the right to vote but being unable to, because there's nowhere one can register to vote in the first place.

Hence this book.

While it is mostly about this power called jingong, there is a deeper underlying current flowing through it like veins in a body nourishing all the vital organs and more.

So without further delay, let us begin.

Chapter Two:

酒

Before I continue, I need to make a couple of points clear.

Firstly, jingong is not a parlour trick in which the process of attaining real jingong can be cheated.

Secondly, anything to do with martial arts takes lots of hard work and years of dedicated persistent practice. True martial arts practice is not an on-off hobby. If you are serious about it, you will do it regardless of the negative shit you got going on in your life.

Thirdly, it is assumed that if you are reading this, then you are actively walking your martial arts path and that the jingong examples given in this book make enough sense for you to realise that this book is just a welcome tavern serving you what you need to keep going.

Fourthly, jingong is like the spirits behind the bar. Some of it is rubbish regardless of the price tag and some of it is top shelf quality stuff. Occasionally you may find a rare gem amongst the cheap stuff and wonder why. But at the end of the day, It is still your choice which bottle you buy.

And lastly, you must remember this. While it may be your choice, the bottle of jingong you ultimately purchase will determine the company you keep.

Most people pick what is popular because they have no genuine way of assessing what is quality and what is not. For a martial artist this is usually because they haven't done enough miles to warrant an adventure in their style. Maybe their Shifu has, but not themselves.

So please, know the company you keep and try to drink responsibly.

Chapter Three:

師

When a person decides to learn the internal martial art of Taichi, they will eventually come across the term: Jingong...

勁功

Much of what is written about it almost doesn't exist. I think, at last count there were in English about three or four books on the subject, with nearly all of them written by one person. While in China, as a martial concept, it is a vague topic that they like to keep as a secret transmission.

However in baguazhang when something is labeled as a secret, it really means that the topic is hard to explain accurately and it is usually inappropriate learning material for a student that only wants to learn how to kick ass and win fights using physical techniques.

But because of who I am and where my journey is leading me, I will explain using modern visualisation techniques what jingong is. Bearing in mind that I have given an explanation before in my podcast numbered 156 on my podcast channel **The Way through Baguazhang**. Only this new example is a better one.

To the Chinese, jin is a very yang, very masculine word. And it has connotations of success, power and force. Whereas qi, it's opposite, would be regarded as being very yin or feminine. Hence most Chinese martial arts do not focus on jin much. Not because jin is a secret but because jin is a given in the style. The problem most styles face is that their jin lies on the surface and hasn't been internalised.

In internally focused martial arts, a truly dedicated practitioner will eventually get to the point where all that internal work, expressed as qigong, suddenly is in need of an external outlet.

The external manifestation of qi is what jin seeks to be.

I guess this next explanation would better explain it: The cultivation of qi through qigong is like building and operating a nuclear power station, with your body being the nearby town that uses the electricity the station provides. So far so good. However, the side effect of having a nuclear power station is that there will be some radioactive byproduct to deal with. And it is what you do with that byproduct that is jingong.

Most martial arts masters will go down the road of inner door secrets, which in this example means having nuclear warheads. Nobody knows that they have them but everybody knows they have them. Whether or not they can actually deploy those weapons is another matter entirely.

For people like me, on the other hand, I see qi like energy being stored in a battery. Once my battery is full, it electromagnetically expands beyond its physical confinement to start filling up the batteries of those around me. It is something like having a strong aura, or even better, being the centre of my very own feng shui map wherever I am.

I could give other examples but this is one of those things you are either gonna "get it" or not, like sex after losing one's virginity.

Chapter Four:

推

I was asked once if a person can have strong jingong without doing any martial arts whatsoever?

And I said yes.

And then I was asked to name at least one type of person with a good grasp of jingong?

And I answered male pornstar.

Yes. The male pornstar. I don't mind letting the pennies drop and losing a few readers, while some angry ones want to challenge me. A truly enlightened disciple would ponder on it for a while, do a few baguazhang sets, meditate on their own understanding of what was said 'before' possibly coming back to me with the follow up question of, so why male pornstars?

And I would reply with thank you for asking, before jumping into another Shifu inspired answer that goes something like this…

Once upon a time, when I got that certain realisation that I didn't know what jingong was, I went on a mission via the internet to find out. And this little grasshopper came up 'crickets'. Hardly anything at all. But then I thought to myself, maybe I am going about this the wrong way. Perhaps I should look for this term using Chinese characters or Japanese kanji. I searched using Chinese traditional and simplified characters and I got assault weapons, heavy construction equipment and some worm screws; in this case, the kanji results were pretty much the same.

When I tried the search again linked to martial arts, jingong only really showed up with Taichi under an even vaguer term of Jinfa. The fa in jinfa is the same 'fa' as in Bingfa or *The Art of War*, with fa meaning law, regulation or method. The Chinese translation of Bingfa more accurately translates as Army Methods, but the more poetic title of The Art of War sells better.

The internet isn't always as all-encompassing as we are geared up to believe. Sometimes it is more of a hindrance than good help. For a lot of things the internet is just endless repetition of the same shallow copy-and-paste information that doesn't mean anything. And so, I asked my wife (who is Chinese) if she has heard of the term jingong. It turns out that in Cantonese she had, and promptly explained how it's commonly used as part of Hong Kong slang. Of which they are all good implications. Except, none of the examples given can easily be translated into a martial setting. Until she explained to me that the real power behind jingong is all about the thrust! A person with good thrusting technique has got good jingong. Hence the male pornstar.

Jingong isn't about the display of power through oversized muscles or even about smashing one's fist through a brick wall. Rather it is about the application of technique so that a minimum of force yields maximum results.

Sadly, most men will be too up themselves to fully appreciate what is being discussed here. But most women will get the gist, even if they abhor pornography. The male pornstar rarely looks like what a man would perceive as being powerful. Most macho guys would dismiss him as an average nobody on the street. And yet, he can do what a lot of men can only wishfully dream about.

Chapter Five:

Honestly, I don't know how the Taichi guys came up with the idea that Jingong is a spiralling type of energy. I, personally, have never experienced it spiralling anything. It just sort of is there, coming and going depending on the size of my proverbial cup.

Most of you by now should be familiar with the proverbial cup: If you want to learn anything, you must first empty your cup.

But did Bruce Lee ever tell anyone what happens, as a matter of experience, when the cup is empty?

I guess not.

Well, here's what happens: You're either broke or at your lowest point or complaining that the dream didn't match what you signed up for. Most of us, who have experienced the pain of having followed his advice, rarely talk about it because it's kind of like a Right of Passage. Oh well... At least now I know another way, a better realised way.

Whatever the size of your initial cup, when a person goes down the internal martial art road, however full your tiny cup may be, the art of cultivating qi actually expands our cup first and then we are able to fill it with new knowledge. Imagine your first cup being the size of a thimble. Whatever was inside, once expanded out to the size of a coffee cup, it will be as good as empty. And once it is full again, the coffee cup will expand again. Maybe this time it is the size of a paint bucket. And on and on it goes.

The process never ends until we choose to stop cultivating our qi.

And so, now that I have told you this, you must be wondering how I know this? I know I would want to know, at least for consistency's sake.

Well I know because it is in my nature to find out and experience it for myself, so that when I talk about it, I am giving the listener firsthand knowledge. It is up to the listener to take what they hear and use it as a comparison to their own experience. It's the listener's choice.

Anyway, it continues on like this: Once your proverbial cup is full with qi, for a brief while it overflows. This overflowing of qi can be summed up as having an abundance of jingong and this is where the magic around us happens. Shit gets done. We're the boss. We da Man. We're Moses in the Land of Milk and Honey. And I know some you know exactly what I mean.

And then, mysteriously, the well seems to go empty and we're back to cultivating our qi again.

We wonder if we had sinned, or abused our powers. How we think about these things depends a lot on our beliefs. We wonder what we did wrong but in truth all that happened was that in the background our cup expanded like a sudden growth spurt. Something likened to running on empty, but that is an illusion.

If this is what has been happening to you, then it is time to start closing the loop so that your jingong cultivation feeds back into your qigong cultivation in a continual cycle. And it starts with realising what is happening.

Chapter Six:

So how does a person know what is happening?

A person will ultimately come to realise what is happening because their intention will tell them so.

In Chinese internal martial arts, the character used for intention is 'yi' and it comes before the process of qi cultivation as a thing in the art. Yi is the idea, wish or desire that empowers you. It is your true 'why' in this case.

That's the theory.

The reality for most people is that, for them, their first meaning of yi, as in idea or meaning, is not in alignment with their secondary meaning of yi as in wish or desire.

It sounds confusing and it is. Much of baguazhang is about figuring out where a person's flow actually resides. And this process takes a long time to get clear on. It is not something a person can master overnight.

And even if a person comes in off the street with a clearly defined goal, usually their true innate goals are not the same. When I first started baguazhang my goals were to improve my health and strengthen my back, while at the same time becoming an awesome kung fu master. Never ever in my wildest dreams would I have picked a goal like being a Living Tao. Or be one to pursue The Way. But this is precisely what powers my jingong.

Another way to look at it is from the angle of quantum physics. In quantum physics, intention is the force by which the mind is able to directly influence its surroundings: Our intentions help us to construct our reality which in turn defines the results we will get. Much of what comes to pass in our lives is decided beforehand and usually without our conscious awareness long before we get to have any physical say in what is happening around us.

For people who insist that being skilled as a fighter gives them a say, the truth couldn't be further away.

Fighting is a direct immediate response to a distressing environment and learning to fight means that the person believes that there are no other options available.

This way of living and thinking is a massive drain on a person's qi reserves. Having an 'accident' that ultimately takes them out of this environment ends up being the blessing they need to find their true path. I am using the word accident very loosely here. It can be anything, actually. But the important thing here is, that once they're out and back in alignment with their true intention or yi, success quickly follows.

It is this success which is a manifestation of their jingong. While most people will try to measure it in terms of material success, jingong isn't the stuff itself. Jingong as a power is measured in the way that stuff is attracted to them – the stronger the qi, the stronger the jin.

And that in a nutshell is the basics around this thing called 'yi' a.k.a. our intentions.

However unless you are into quantum physics or are into the spiritual side of things, this next bit will be a little harder to appreciate. When we have a strong or clearly defined intention, we are actually energetically projecting out into the distant future of what we want to happen.

And this is where we need to get clear on what we are signing up for. Most people adamantly will argue until the cows come home that they know what they are going for, but as soon as the physical reality of that goal becomes manifest, they start getting cold feet.

For example, a lot of westerners brought up on martial arts movies have the fantasy of being an A grade awesome take-no-shit street fighter.

While the fantasy is one thing, in order to make it an everyday reality, the environment in which a person lives in must also be of such a nature that being a street fighter is the norm, as an everyday occurrence.

So let's just say for a moment that you don't want to live a life in which every single day you're out on the streets fighting, then how does a person know what their true yi or intention is?

Figuring it out is what part of the journey is about.

We assume that there is someone near us who has their life all worked out and has all the answers. Maybe you got lucky and you do. But chances are, their life is not your life. And even if they have tried to guide you, you probably weren't listening.

At other times, we are listening but the messages are puzzling. In this case it could be puzzling because in basic Anglo-Saxon English, the word 'yi' also means 'the will' as in a person's willpower.

We are, these days, taught that the will is to be seen as an aggressive negative quality until, of course, a person has made it and then the will miraculously becomes one's force of nature. Unless it has something to do with sports, a person's will is meant to stay hidden. Which is just another version of the master and slave dance routine.

In baguazhang the will is a fundamental tenant that bridges the gap between mind (Shen) and energy (Qi). Malleable metal doesn't just bend because it is softer or weaker than the force (Li) applied to it. Although that has a lot to do with it. A lot of malleable metals are thus, because one's will makes it so. Being physically harder is not always better. There will be times in a person's life where the will

(Yi) is the only thing capable of making things happen.

In practical terms, the power of yi is to keep the mind steady and clear when everything around it wants to drown it in trivial bullshit. Which is vital when cultivating one's qi to the mass required to have jin.

To give an example, I'm actually not that big. My physique and height is average but my yi is like stone. During the COVID-19 pandemic, a lot of countries went into lockdown in which most people were forced to stay at home. But in Australia, people were allowed the option of going out to pick up their online orders from shops instead of having it couriered for a fee to their home. Now as it just so happens, I have great customer relations skills over and above the call of duty, and so my company placed me at the front door where customers come to pick up their orders. Apart from knowing how to successfully handle customers, they have me there because my will or yi is such that when I say yes, it is yes and when I say no, it is no. Just like Saint Peter at the Gates of Heaven.

But there's also a downside with yi. The more determined it becomes, the more it will attract that which seeks to challenge it. For me, in my example, that would be some of the customers. It's not that they mean to give me shit. Many of them are not even aware that they are doing it. If they had been consciously aware of it, they'd probably stop. So I just roll with the punches and win.

It's the tiny few who bring out the viciousness in me that I'm most concerned about. Because they allow me to override my saintliness for a more brutal personification.

Anyway, while I might have digressed there a bit, your yi is your intention, idea, will. It is your "Why are you even reading this book?"

Chapter Seven:

The hardest parts to grasp regarding jingong are:

1) It is for most martial artists uncharted waters. While it appears to be the external side of the internal workings of qigong, it is not the same thing as training in a hard or externally focused martial art. And;

2) Depending on your style of martial art, your path towards understanding jingong will be completely different to somebody schooled in another style. I do baguazhang, so that means my comprehension of it will be through baguazhang.

My role as a "Living Tao" is to give enough insights, so that if you come across this podcast or one of my books, you will get a sense of where you are headed.

Your own experience of it is vital if you want to master it. So don't dismiss or discount your own personal martial history because your naysayers don't want the same thing.

Actually, it's not even that. What is really happening is reality is catching up with them, when it comes to you, and suddenly they are getting that nagging feeling that they are being left behind.

For you see, while a person is doing qigong or an internally focused martial art, it is easy to dismiss it all as just fooling around, no matter how serious the practitioner may be. It's like they can only see the toddler in the sandbox playing with his Matchbox cars, even though the toddler is a teenager surfing around on the beach. That so-called toddler has moved up and is about to leave the beach for the desert. And his toy car is now a real Toyota Landcruiser.

Jingong is a massive scaling up from qigong. It has to be. Because in a strange and weird sort of way, it's no longer just about the self. It is about the self in context to its surroundings. In other words: Fengshui.

A person with jingong can move to an alien environment and within a very short period of time, that environment will start changing to reflect them in subtle ways. Even if the whole process can be denied, if their jingong is strong enough, the people around them will start to notice the changes. And they will usually have people around them comment like this, “How come, or why is it, that whenever you go somewhere, XYZ starts appearing around you?” Or, “Where’d all these XYZ people come from? We never had them, but now you are here and they’re everywhere — it’s like you bought your whole damn tribe with you?”

If something like this has ever happened to you then, firstly, congratulations. You got strong jingong. And, secondly, that so-called tribe isn’t your family as in blood relations. No. They reflect the ancestral lineage of the martial art you have been marinating in.

At the same time this is going on, things that are not aligned with your qi start disappearing from your life. I know some of you will want to nervously laugh and mock, because it is touching on one’s self identity. But this is the meaning behind Pak Tai, the Dark Warrior washing his guts clean in the river (before ascending Wudang Mountain).

For those of you, who need a monotheistic explanation: Qigong is the process by which the martial artist uses the body to burn off the sins polluting their soul. While baptism and holy water works for some people on an external level, the process of qigong is internal and goes much deeper. It acknowledges before God that this process of cleaning one's soul is the same as walking and breathing. Nobody can do it for you. You have to do it by yourself. Amen.

Chapter Eight:

焰

Since my most recent podcasts about jingong came to air, I have been requested to give a practical example of how jingong works; for the less spiritually inclined.

For the briefest of moments, this got me thinking. And I got the feeling that maybe, just maybe, I might be overthinking it a bit.

And as it turns out, I was overthinking it. Because after I received the request, it just so happened that on social media there is a video clip going around that shows jingong clearly.

And get this: The rebuttal video that is also circulating around, also is a very good example of jingong.

The first video shows a person trying to blow out a candle flame using either their palm or fist from a few inches away with a straight forward thrusting motion. It looks a little like the one-inch punch, but the palm or fist never touches the candle flame.

This exercise, if done correctly, teaches the mind to focus on a small target that has the ability to shift its station (by flickering). In other words the flame can move about. One's qi in this case, is literally the pocket of air between the candle flame and the person's hand. When the hand moves forward, it pushes the air in front (of it) forward, which in turn snuffs out the flame.

It seems easy to do, but it is actually quite hard to master because if the mind dithers, the hand wavers, and the air in front goes everywhere except where it's supposed to. Which is to blow out the candle flame.

The jingong part is the air moving in the right intended direction towards the target to have an effect on the situation.

If you are practicing with one of those magic birthday candles that never seem to go out, this exercise is even more difficult to master.

And the rebuttal video?

Well, it basically just shows a guy blowing out the candle the old-fashioned way: Inhale air into the mouth and then exhale! And wallah, the candle flame is blown out. Again, if qi is just air and breathing, the sucking in and out part would be qigong, while the air moving to its intended effect will be jingong.

What people fail to appreciate is that blowing out a candle flame is a practiced skill that most people started doing since they had to make a wish and blow that damn birthday candle out. Now it should be easy-peasy at our age, but there is always that someone who upturns our assumptions because they can't blow out a simple little candle.

And, while these two examples given, may seem like a simple case of basic 'cause and effect', it is only the air being pushed forward or blown out that is the cause and the candle flame blowing out is the effect. In baguazhang, a true master of jingong will understand before any action has been undertaken, that once the candle is blown out, the final environmental state will be darkness.

Most people will only comprehend the darkness because they are in the moment of experiencing it. They will not know that the darkness is just an after-effect of the candle going out. This is why it is vital to get one's intent straight. With a clear intention a practitioner will be able to sense which their qi is progressing and in turn come to understand better how their jingong affects the world around them.

Chapter Nine:

鞭

It's funny how when a person focuses on something with determined dedication, certain things have a way of just showing up, as if left at one's front door. It's like the gods are watching and they like what they see.

While it didn't quite happen this way, you could say that Baguazhang Soft Snake Whip Jingong makes a nice addition to this book because it is a form of baguazhang internal skill training, which is usually learnt after a practitioner has mastered a certain amount of foundational work that includes, but is not limited by, the walking of the circle and some of the simple palm changes.

Please note that when practicing any form of internalising work, particular attention must be given to remaining simple and unpretentious in movement. This is so that the mind and body can be free to focus on the subtleties of internal martial arts theory.

When practicing Soft Snake Whip Jingong, a practitioner must avoid using any kind of hard force as this can cause a body's movements to go stiff and unwieldy. Rather it is ideal to seek the softness within a snake's movements.

When beginning to learn this type of jingong exercise, start off with slow movements. At first it will take some time for a practitioner to find their inner spirit, for it is this inner spirit that will gradually help to replace any stiffness within the body with a calm attitude. And ironically, it is this calm attitude that will actually speed up the transition from stiffness to where one's qi flows endlessly like a torrential dragon river even though the mind remains calm and steady.

While most people who come across this chapter will be wondering if it is some kind of special Kung fu move or secret transition from master to disciple, it is nothing like that. Rather, it is rarely practiced because it is difficult to practice even though it can be done by walking the circle very slowly or sitting in the cross-legged meditation position. To do it well, a baguazhang practitioner, before beginning, should have a calm heart and lacking impatience.

Essentially it is still the baguazhang you know but it is primarily the nature of the training a practitioner does that undergoes change.

The Baguazhang Soft Snake Whip Jingong

1) With a calm heart and free of impatience, training will shift from daylight towards evenings. In the days before electricity and light bulbs, evening was the time people naturally started to wind down in preparation for bedtime. Candle light or retro-tungsten lighting will help to set the right mood if one needs, for whatever reason, extra lighting. The strongest results seem to occur when the night is darkest. Why this should be, nobody knows.

2) As a person is in sitting meditation or doing their baguazhang circle walking, one's breathing should be focused on cultivating their qi as if it is flowing around the whole body. The mind will wander hither-thither, so it is important to keep one's yi or intention focused on what their qi is supposed to be doing.

3) Do not force results. Remember to stay calm and let things be as they are. As you let things just be as they are, a practitioner's breath will gradually start to show signs of strength in it. This is the 'whipping' part of the exercise's name.

4) If one is in a sitting meditation, one should visualise with their breathing as if they are riding a boat down a river that alternates from a steady flow to sometimes being a white water rapid.

5) On the other hand, if the practitioner has decided to do their baguazhang form, then they should focus their mind on the movements of a snake as it cuts through the grass or around branches in search of its next meal. It is the focusing on the snake and it's movements that gives us the 'snake' part in the title.

6) Remember to stay as soft as possible in one's movements. There is sometimes a tendency in the visualisation to get over excited and this can lead to wanting to forcibly control what is happening, even though in reality nothing is physically happening as such.

7) Enjoy the internal view. Enjoy what is happening.

8) If you are doing this exercise in the evenings, remember to get plenty of rest during the daytime on the following day, as you may experience your body wanting to purge itself of toxins.

9) Remember that different places have different snakes. Focus on the one that is most aligned to your inner nature. Usually during the exercise, if you don't try to force anything, it will reveal itself in your mind's eye.

Remember, while there may be a tendency to ask, "Is that it?" This exercise is actually quite hard to master because it is not just about daydreaming about snakes.

People who muck around with it, usually get a fleeting feeling of seeing shadows where there are no shadows. And that is because in general, baguazhang and all the other internal martial arts are also about fighting using your mind. Martial arts is also an Art of War, and soldiers never tire of deception. The palms of baguazhang are meant to be soft and slippery, and where the palms can 'slip' there is deception. And through slippage, the enemy can be defeated. The act of turning the palms is also the act of turning the mind. While walking the circle is a form of walking wisdom.

Chapter Ten:

Sometimes the jin of jingong is called martial power or Fa Jin, which translates as 'emitting power or force'.

If you come across this term in your training, then it will usually be a yardstick of what a superior baguazhang master is supposed to have or use during a fight. And it is meant to manifest when the master strikes their opponent.

Unlike true jingong which has a holistic influence over the surrounding environment, Fa Jin is a concentration of power designed to ensure maximum impact on a specific target without using too much physical strength.

Both jingong and Fa Jin are externalizations of one's qi. But that is where the similarities end.

Fa Jin is usually spoken fondly of by practitioners seeking to level the playing field, when there is a clear physical disadvantage against them by a stronger or more skilled opponent. It has been likened to gently tapping an opponent, while the opponent experiences it as being smashed with a sledgehammer!

I won't go into too much further detail regarding Fa Jin, as you can get a lot of information on it already. And it is not the subject of this book.

However, while the power of Fa Jin sounds awesome, eventually a true master of baguazhang will have to confront the violence and harm to others being wrought through its use. If used over a long period of time, there usually is a payback that the master will have to deal with. The original masters used to say that the price paid was the depletion of one's qi and could lead to the practitioner's death when all their qi was gone.

Thankfully, most masters skilled in using Fa Jin, end up shunning its use for violence and instead seek to use it for healing. Because the art of healing transcends the art of violence. For most beginners this idea is usually thought of as a paradox. Of which it is. But unusually, when a practitioner gets here, the paradoxical nature of learning violence in order to heal also makes sense.

When we truly stop for a moment to think about it, almost all acts of violence are born out of suffering which in turn is born out of something broken. Would it not be better to just fix what's broken in the first place?

Jingong, neither really harms nor heals. But rather as an extension of one's internal qigong, it simply changes the environment to what one needs in order to live in harmony with one's surroundings.

When Fa Jin is used as a healing art, the practitioner through touch uses their qi to assist their patience's own healing abilities. It's not a miracle cure or wonder drug, as the patient must first be willing to accept the offer of help. Without that willingness or acceptance, qi cannot flow from practitioner to patient at the point of physical contact.

While I do not regard myself as a healer, in my own experience, when my qi flows out of my hands and into the other person's body, I sometimes get an instantaneous sense of what is wrong and at other times nothing. Usually through employing pressure hands, my qi assists the patient's own recovery by causing the polluting qi to come out. I usually, jokingly, refer to it as an oil change or an engine flush.

The downside for me, sometimes, is that some of that polluting qi backflows into me. And I can spend a day or two being quite sick.

You'd think in this modern world that people would in general be healthier than their forebears. And maybe this was the case a couple decades ago. But nowadays, I sense in most people only the external appearance of being healthy. Internally most people are quite sick. And it's all the usual causes. Worse still, their attitude towards health is that it is the responsibility of other people who are supposed to save them while they continue to enjoy the life that's destroying their health. Hence, I opt out of helping most people. They have to figure this out for themselves.

I know that what I am saying can seemingly be contradictory to me being a "Living Tao", but it is not. There is a massive difference between being asked, "Can you save me, while I continue to do the opposite?" And, "I know I messed up, but can you point me to the doctors?"

Chapter Eleven:

道

Taoism is a form of spiritual philosophy rooted strongly in the ways of nature. If you were to ask me, after having read all my stuff, am I a Taoist? I would have to ponder on it. I sound like a Taoist. I think and act like a Taoist. And I even have to varying degrees have the life of a Taoist. But when I look at the trappings of what makes a true Taoist, I would answer the question with a no.

I know this sounds strange. And it is to me too. Whenever I study the subject, I feel like I do not measure up. It's a bit like telling people you're a devout Christian but you never go to church on Sundays and follow the rites. Things just don't square up for most people.

And yet, through the I-Ching, baguazhang and qigong, to name just a few, I have walked a parallel life to the Taoist teachings.

For a long time I did not understand why this would be so, but now I have come to realise that there are many paths to the Tao and baguazhang is one of them.

Baguazhang has its own way of getting there. The Tao is welcoming to all who seek it. Not that we are trying to seek it, because walking the circle is already a physical expression of the Tao itself. We need not go anywhere to be one with it. It is right here as we do our forms.

While Taoism has its three treasures: Jing, Qi, Shen and is the way through inner alchemy to finding enlightenment, baguazhang also has its treasures. These baguazhang treasures are Shen, Yi, Qi, and Li.

Shen means spirit.
Yi means intention or will.
Qi means energy or life force.
Li means physical power.

The jing of Taoism which means 'essence' as in a person's sexual fluids does not get much of a mention in baguazhang. And this is because in baguazhang, when a person is the process of cultivating one of the treasures, there is part of it that requires the person to live the life of having that treasure at its most powerful, at its weakest, when it makes no difference to one's life and when it manifests at its most ideal state, so that the baguazhang practitioner can truly understand, like the Tao itself, what this treasure actually is.

Suppressing one's Jing in order to guard it from wasteful depletion in the hopes of extending one's life, is no different to living an over-sexed life. Both extremes are focused on the crotch. And both extremes have a tendency to make one open to corruption. The Baguazhang masters realised very early on, that a lot of young men's aggression was led by having too much Jing. And having too much Jing made them poor candidates for the true arts.

The other thing to watch out about Jing is that in Putonghua Mandarin, Jing and Jin sound the same to a westerner's ears. And at times they can be spelt exactly the same. It is always good practice to get the Chinese characters as well, so there is no confusion as to which Jing or Jin is being discussed.

At other times like Shen, it is the exact same character for both treasure sets, but the meaning changes to varying degrees. Shen in baguazhang refers more to a practitioner's soul, while in Taoist alchemy it leans more to the meaning of one's mind or consciousness. A lot of times these definitions can also interchange depending on the lesson or situation. It is never a clear cut thing. Even the idea of Shen meaning soul, at times can be incorrect. Sometimes Shen just means spirit.

Without the living experience of these treasures, transcendence can be painstakingly slow.

However, once the experience has been lived through, things seem to just quantum leap up to the next stage as if it has always been a part of one's life.

The thing to remember about jingong is is that your qi is no longer just an individual internal matter. Your qi is now affecting everything outside of you as well. And as such, your environment and everything within it is also becoming a part of you. In Taoist alchemy they lump all this in with cultivating one's Shen. And there is a tendency to remind the cultivator that while they are cultivating their Shen, they are not immortal or enlightened.

Baguazhang takes a slightly different view. By calling it jingong, they see it as just another stage to becoming enlightened. Not necessarily the big Buddha spiritual one, but closer towards the path of self-realisation which has got nothing to do with other people telling them how it's meant to be. If it is about becoming a Taoist immortal, then that path is a private affair between the baguazhang practitioner and the Tao.

Ultimately it is not about necessarily attaining immortality. It is about the path itself. That is the Way. Any roadblocks can be swiftly dealt with using the fixed or changing palms.

Chapter Twelve:

By now, if you had been reading this book, you might be wondering how jingong relates to war (other than making a snappy title)?

To answer that question, imagine a person living in a constant state of war. And somehow, while in a constant state of war, they have managed to find the time and space to cultivate their qi through some form of qigong or neigong work.

At some point, having done all this cultivation, they would come to the realisation, which is a form of enlightenment, that their qi extends beyond their physical body. And as such, their qi which externally is their jin would quite naturally start influencing their surroundings. Maybe not actively at least at first, but as a side-effect of qigong.

A person living in such a constant state of war would find it quite natural to have a warlike state of mind. Even if he or she were a pacifist, their words and frames of reference would have a strong modelling through the framework of war.

While thankfully most people are blessed enough to not have to live like that, there is still enough aggression in western i.e. American dominated culture for people to act and think as if they were.

You can see it in their obsession with tactical this or tactical that. And learning a form of martial art that outside of practice, they will never need to use. It's all pretend soldiering designed to inflate the ego and it has got nothing to do with self-defence or truly protecting those we love.

For me, whenever I am doing baguazhang, I am simultaneously doing qigong as well, and as a further result I am also doing jingong. My jingong is strong. Very strong. So strong in fact that my thoughts, feelings and actions have a real physical effect on a vast area of my dominion.

What that means in relation to this chapter is that while it appears that I am 'lording it' over my turf like some petty baron, I get to quietly through my jingong mold the feng shui so that it flows in a more auspicious alignment that protects what needs protecting, within my sphere of influence without having to constantly go to war to achieve it.

Nobody is forced to do anything while within my sphere of influence except naturally being in harmony with what I am. For most people it means that while they may not fully grasp what is going on when they are near me, they get a bit of my qi brushing off on them.

If on the other hand for whatever reason a person is not in alignment with my area's feng shui, then they simply, of their own volition, leave. No force is ever used. They simply get a sense that this area isn't right for them. And I support their decision.

I do not expect you to believe what I tell you, but I am not the first martial arts master to have experienced this. A lot of western martial artists don't realise this, but when the ancient kung fu texts or stories got translated, there was usually a passage that got omitted. And it went something like this: XYZ master of XYZ style lived in XYZ town/village and the feng shui was very good.

It is sometimes assumed that the master went to live in a place with excellent feng shui. But that is not how it worked. The master went to the town first and then, through his qigong and then jingong cultivation, the town's feng shui improved.

If a feng shui master were to visit the town, they would realise very quickly, by the lack of physical evidence that another source was giving the town good feng shui. Upon investigation they would eventually come to realise the kung fu master's influence.

This influence or expression of power is called shi or shih. And is spoken about a lot in Suntzu's classic Bingfa or The Art of War.

Because most martial artists shut their ears when the language gets too flowery. And want to feel strong and powerful, not soft and gentle, I strongly recommend that they make a sincere effort to read The Art of War. Which was intended to be read by kings and generals alike. If this is still too much then I don't know what will help you to get over your ignorance other than direct experience.

Chapter Thirteen:

力

Sometimes you hear jingong being split into two types: Bright and Dark. As in what can and cannot be seen by the eyes, and not as is usually first assumed to mean good and evil.

When it is split as such, then it is more of a Taichi phenomenon. In Baguazhang this does not refer to jingong but Li which means power as in muscular power (Refer back to Chapter Eleven).

When researching on bright or dark jin, you will usually hear or read stories about great kung fu masters having electricity in their arms or when attacked able to mysteriously repel advances by simply blocking.

But the truth is a lot simpler to understand if I use the sport of weightlifting to explain it.

Bright jin in weightlifting are those guys with giant muscles. Bright means being able to see the power or force being used. Big muscles means being able to lift heavy weights. In martial arts bright jin is all those guys punching and kicking and smashing bricks. You get the idea. It's out there for all to see.

Dark jin in weightlifting are those tiny guys who engage in the sport of powerlifting. By just looking at them, you would never know their true strength, and if it were told to you, you probably would not believe it. And the reason is because what you see in muscles does to match one's perceived concept of big powerful muscles. But once they get on stage and do their powerlift, it's game over. What they are able to deadlift smashes whatever claims bright jin guys have.

In Taichi, dark jin is the power to hurt your opponent by only blocking because one's bones, sinew and muscles are that much stronger at its most basic level.

At a higher level, it is the ability to reflect back onto the attacker the attacker's own force amplified. Many internal martial art practitioners, if they are aware of this, seek to attain it because it allows them to be powerful without exposing themselves to unnecessary provocations. In other words: Outwardly weak while internally strong.

An advanced baguazhang practitioner, on the other hand, will through practice begin to appreciate the subtle mechanics that the body is able to do. While most training is done through utilising the fixed palms and internal strength training, a lot of Li (physical power) comes from how energy mechanically flows through the body.

To give an example, if my opponent were to try and punch me but I managed to block with a simple forearm block, I would probably need to use greater force than my opponent to achieve my defensive aims. Usually the only way to get around this would require me to go through extensive muscle and bone conditioning of a greater magnitude than whatever my opponent can throw at me.

However due to the unique properties of muscle and sinew mechanics, I know that if I can twist my forearm at moment of impact, muscle and sinew tightening would occur, thereby giving the same rock hard resistance as if I had conditioned my forearms by smashing them against a brick wall or something. Untwist a split moment later and the concentrated energy at point of impact would naturally disperse and dissipate through one's body.

It sounds miraculous but to be able to automatically do it, takes years of dedicated practice. It's an acquired skill that has to be drilled into the body and mind.

The electrical sensation that opponents sometimes experience at the moment of impact, is the baguazhang master combining Li (muscular power) with their internal qi through the art of Yi (intention or will) to achieve their aims. Which is to give back tenfold!

If you don't believe this, then just think of it this way instead: Imagine the attack being a drummer hitting a drum with a certain amount of force. Understanding Li (muscular power) is knowing that the stretched piece of animal skin over the barrel hole will produce a certain kind of amplified sound. An experienced drummer will have a very good idea of what kind of drum will produce what kind of sound at what kind of volume depending on how he hits it.

Dark jin's advantage is that the opponent is unaware of any of this because the usual signs are missing or more accurately hidden.

Now through science and engineering, these same results can be secretly implemented without too much fuss, but a lot of traditional kung fu masters view it as cheating. Sometimes though, the smarter way is to be pragmatic about it. Catching flying arrows at twenty yards might be a really cool feat to master, but it might be a wiser investment to wear a bulletproof vest when dealing with guns.

Chapter Fourteen:

流

As you can probably guess, Chapter Thirteen wasn't really about true jingong. You will, if you dig deep enough, find a lot of other terms attached to jin. And it will appear at first glance to have something to do with jingong. But it's all about the power.

True jingong is not a secret.

Jingong is what happens when qigong cultivation stops being an internal affair, and a person's qi starts to directly influence their external surroundings.

Until now this concept around energy has been poorly defined as far as baguazhang is concerned. Other forms of martial arts have got their own paths to follow.

It is hoped that after you have read this book, and not just glanced through it, that you will have a much clearer understanding of what it is jingong.

However, it sometimes does not matter what I or anyone else says, there will always be people who will not believe a single word of it. They are usually looking for something that they cannot find because they are usually looking for it in the wrong place.

If you are having trouble believing, put the book down. And let it go. Go give it to someone who actually enjoys this kind of internal energy work.

Why keep struggling with something that you do not enjoy?

But what if you are like so many people out there who secretly want what I am teaching, but publicly amongst their peers reject this stuff about jingong outright?

Well, then, I am sad to say that you will not get what you are seeking at this point in time.

This is because everything that you are experiencing right now is a direct result of the thoughts you've been having up till now. Those same thoughts have been powering your intentions (see Chapter Six) and in turn those intentions have been fueling your cultivation of qi. In other words, you've been expecting your qi to flow a certain way that remains in harmony with the company you keep. And so that is how you will continue to get it into the foreseeable future. Unless something is done to change the direction of one's flow of qi.

Chapter Fifteen:

It may be a bit presumptuous of me, but throughout this book it has been assumed that the reader knows something about qi and qigong. And while I have throughout this book directly or indirectly made comments around the subject, I have been informed that I have not actually addressed it. Especially since it is the third baguazhang treasure, with the first being Shen, second Yi and the fourth one being Li.

After much contemplation I have to ask, what possibly could I say that isn't already covered by my book **The Baguazhang Qigong Illustrated through 64 I-Ching inspired postures**?

Not much really, if anything at all.

If you are already a practitioner of qigong, you are not going to need further words to explain what you already know.

If you are not a practitioner of qigong, no amount of further explaining, is going to improve your non-existing practice.

And if you are just starting, your bridge to comprehension will usually be a teacher or instructor of the skill. Words will usually be an immediate direct transmission from master to disciple during class time, where its impact on learning is the most effective.

What is important to practitioners of qigong is knowing how to gauge when the practice of qigong (internal) is now the practice of jingong (external).

And that's the tricky part.

Sometimes the line that separates the two is a feeling. At other times it is a thought. And then there are those moments that would best be described as a kind of realisation. It all depends on the person and their personal measurement of what makes an event definite. For a lot of people that 'something' needs to be a physical external event. Which is only a natural stage of development.

Baguazhang is no exception.

There are the external milestones: Improved health; better coordination; hopefully also better at fighting and so on. And then there are the half/half milestones that come next: Improved defence; more spatially aware; it becomes a way of life. And then you have the internal milestones: Baguazhang is qigong; improved intuition skills; plus a host of others that can't be spelt out here because they fall under the category of 'Private Stuff - Mind Your Own Business!'

Actually, that last bit is actually quite important. So much of the art is just that: Minding one's business. Both literally and figuratively.

I guess when we get to that stage where we realise that we are minding our own business, is the stage when we know that we have crossed the river. Our cultivation of qi is now the cultivation of jin.

In short, you just know.

Chapter Sixteen:

巫

So far, throughout this book I have tried as best as I could to keep an even keel as we sail through the mysteries of jingong. But now it is time for the logically minded to take a break. Put the book down for a day. And after skipping Chapter Sixteen, maybe resume its contents in the next chapter.

This chapter is for the spiritually inclined.

If you find yourself reading this chapter and wanting to mock or argue, then there are some things around baguazhang that you will find the door closed to you. But, if you have a strong leaning towards the spiritual, many of the higher divine concepts around baguazhang will be like a homecoming. I have not forgotten you.

Some of you will have noticed that when you are doing baguazhang forms, and in particular the fixed palms, occasionally it can feel like a dance.

And when those same forms are further practiced to music, usually to help with tempo or flow, it can feel as if we are missing a partner. It's as if there should be two people facing each other as we move in synchronicity around the bagua circle. Indeed some styles of baguazhang have this kind of circle walking as part of their training regime.

The reason for this sensation is because at its very core, the roots of baguazhang are shamanistic. To be a baguazhang master is to be a shaman.

Not the cliqued drum banging hippie who has gone native and wants to heal everything, love everything and occasionally use it as an excuse to smoke weed, but the real thing.

Those who are spiritually inclined will eventually at some point in their training, find themselves practicing in near dark lighting while listening to mood music that has the effect of putting themselves in a trancelike state. It's almost like a calling to be closer to the divine.

If this has ever happened to you, then without realising it, you were in your own way doing the baguazhang soft snake whip jingong. I know because I went down that road. And when I had completed the form I found myself face to face with a giant black snake whose head was as big as my own. For a moment we stared at each other and then it was gone. The snake in many ancient cultures is associated with healing and wisdom. And the main totemic emblem of baguazhang is the snake. That is why there is a Swimming Dragon Form.

Yes, it's called Swimming Dragon, and yes we are referring to the Celestial Chinese Dragon, but calling something 'dragon' in Chinese is also poetic licence for snake and anything else with a similar shape or profile like comets, swords and penises. Just as a Chinese dish called phoenix something or other is just chicken.

Why this all matters is because as we get stronger with our jingong and how it is manifested outwards into our environment, that which cannot exist in our reality gets pushed out (spiritually speaking) as if our reality is guarded by our totemic snake.

Another way to understand it is that we get compared to snakes and the type of snake we get compared to is our totem.

It's not just in the way we move but also in the way we do things. And in particular how we choose to fight our battles. Master Dong Hai Chuan was sometimes said to move like a viper against his opponents. While other masters were compared to other various snakes. I myself am usually compared to the boa constrictor: Slow, steady, relentless. And only striking as a last resort.

Anyway, the point of this chapter isn't about how to fight like a snake. A shaman doing the rain dance, if possible, would be a far more useful skill to have, especially living in such a hot continent like Australia. I mean, look at the Rainbow Serpent. After it finished creating everything in the Dreamtime, did it go off and make war?

No.

It left us billabongs (natural watering holes) all over the place to help everything out.

Chapter Seventeen:

勁

If you took my advice and skipped Chapter Sixteen, welcome back.

On the night I finished writing that chapter, it just so happened that Sydney was struck by a major supercell storm. The whole thunder and lightning works. It was spectacular with actual lightning bolts hitting the ground. Usually they just race across the sky. I think the last similar type of storm was about four years ago when a bolt struck the Baulkham Hill shopping mall and plunged it into darkness for several hours. What was even more impressive was the fact that I was driving to that mall when it happened. Luckily I got to the mall just before the thunder and lightning was followed by a major hailstorm. It is never a good idea to be out and about when they hit. Sometimes the hail can be large enough to write off cars.

And so, with the latest storm I watched it from the safety of my home before going to bed for the evening. I fell asleep and the next morning I woke up refreshed with one of the best dreams I have ever had.

Ever since I started writing this book, I have been having dreams of unrecognisable kung fu masters coming to challenge my authority on baguazhang. Not like in the martial art movies where the protagonist isn't allowed to teach unless he pays the grandmaster's 'tuition fees' but more of a test of my abilities. Sometimes these tests appear more like a strange paradoxical maze that I must get through than a martial bout.

But this last dream was the best because in it I met Kwan Yin the Goddess of Mercy and we strolled together through one of her fabled gardens. It was peaceful and beautiful. And while nothing much happened in the dream, I am left with a feeling of contentment and knowing that essentially this book is complete and finished.

I know that there will always be people who will feel that it is never enough, but this is Kwan Yin we are talking about and she takes precedence. Jingong is what it is.

I AM A LIVING TAO FOR MYSELF AND OTHERS ALONG THIS MARTIAL ARTS WAY. Blessings blessings blessings to all who cross my path.

www.ingramcontent.com/pod-product-compliance
Ingram Content Group UK Ltd.
Pitfield, Milton Keynes, MK11 3LW, UK
UKHW021931200726
13853UKWH00010B/58